Al, the lifeguard, hears some
Look at the pictures and tell

1

Say the name of the picture.
Listen to the sound of the first letter. Write the letter.

2

The pictures in each row tell a story. They are not in order.
Draw an X on the picture that comes first.

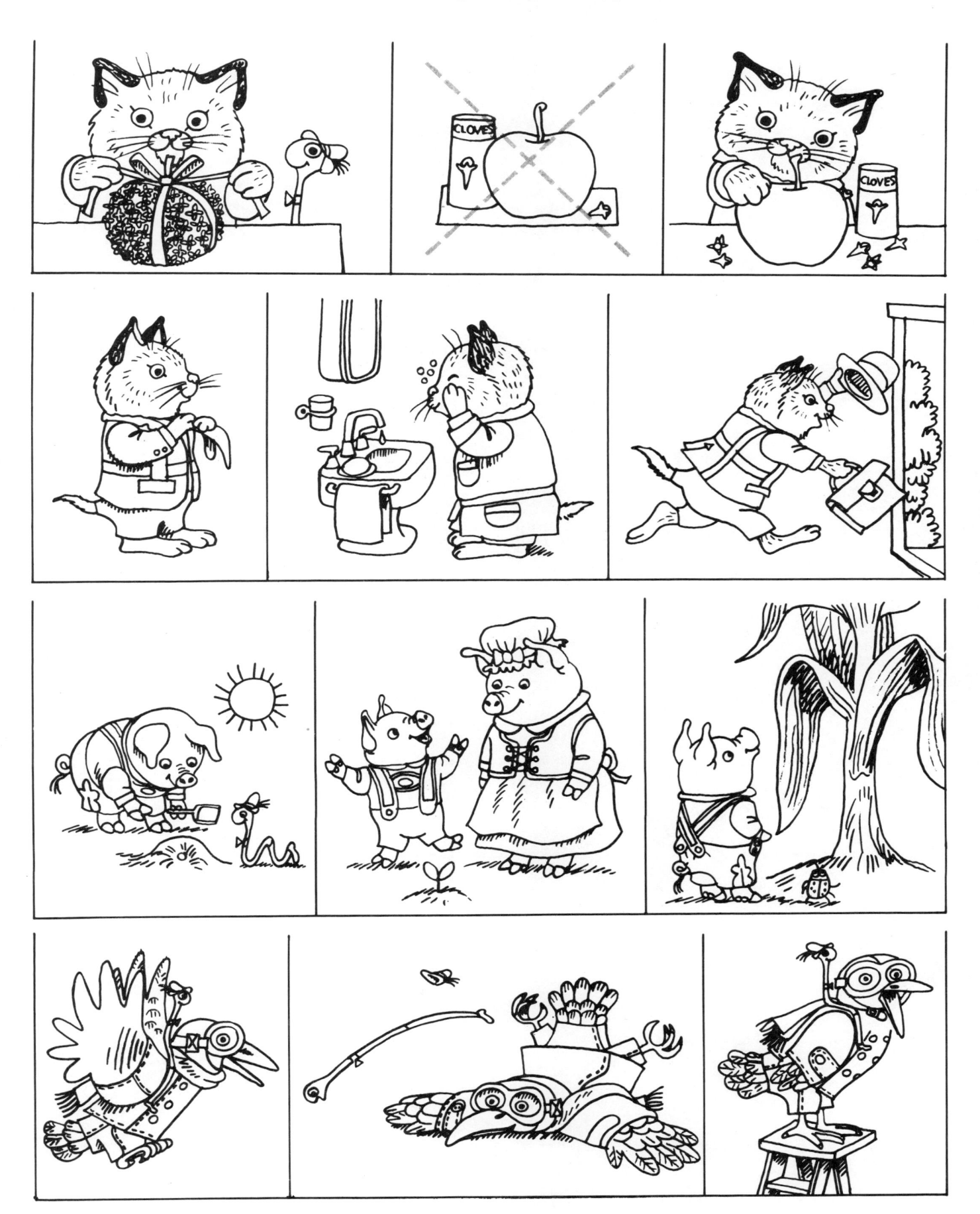

**Say the name of the picture.
Listen to the sound of the first letter. Write the letter.**

The pictures in each row tell a story. They are not in order.
Draw an X on the one that should come last.

5

Make the sound of the small letters. Write the letters.

a e i o u

a

Say the name of the picture.
Write a middle letter from the box above to complete the word.

h e n   s   x   l   g

c   t   m   g   j   t

f _ sh   b _ g   b _ s

b _ rn   s l _ d   s _ nk

d _ st   h _ t   d _ g

Say the words. Listen to the last sound.
The words have the same ending sound.

broom   drum

Say the word for each picture. Draw an X on the picture that ends with the same sound as the one in the box.

map	leak	mop
net	bird	hat
fox	crab	axe

Draw an X on the pictures that have the same ending sound in each row.

| bush | fish | drink | splash |

| doll | raft | bell | ball |

| five | shell | wave | stove |

| fork | cake | bike | scooter |

The children are having a picnic.
Help Lowly find his way to the hot dog.
Help Little Sister find her way to the ice cream cone.

Draw a line under the words that rhyme in each row.

coat	goat	boat	bell
log	dog	fish	frog
stick	stove	chick	sick
mow	row	barrel	sew
rink	farmer	sink	drink

Write the missing letters.

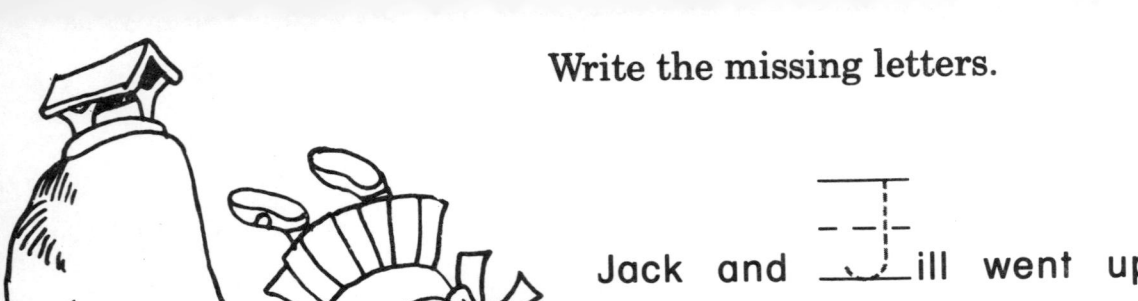

Jack and **J**ill went up the **h**ill

To __f__etch a __p__ail of water;

Jack fell down and broke his __c__rown,

And Jill came tumbling __a__fter.

Georgie Porgie, pudding and __p__ie,

Kissed the __g__irls and made them __c__ry;

When the boys came out to __p__lay,

Georgie Porgie __r__an away.

Draw an X on the pictures that rhyme in each row.

sled   bag   bed   head

hen   pen   tape   ten

rug   mug   kettle   bug

dig   pig   medal   wig

sun   mask   run   one

Read the words. Say the words. Write the words.

The	The	Has	Has	A	A
the	the	has	has	a	a

The [cat] has a [bat].

The cat has a bat.

The cat has a [book].

The cat has a book.

The [book] has a book.

Read the words. Say the words. Write the words.

Can _Can_ can _can_ and _and_

The pig can dig.

The pig can dig.

The cat and the pig.

The cat and the pig can dig.

Can the cat and the pig dig?

Read the words. Say the words. Write the words.

Run *Run* run *run*

The [dog] can run.
dog

The *dog* can run.

The cat,

the pig,

and the dog can run.

Fun, *fun*, fun!

Can the hat run? *No*

Read the words. Colour the picture.
Colour all spaces that say red with a red crayon.
Colour all spaces that say blue with a blue crayon.
Colour all spaces that say yellow with a yellow crayon.
Colour all spaces that say green with a green crayon.

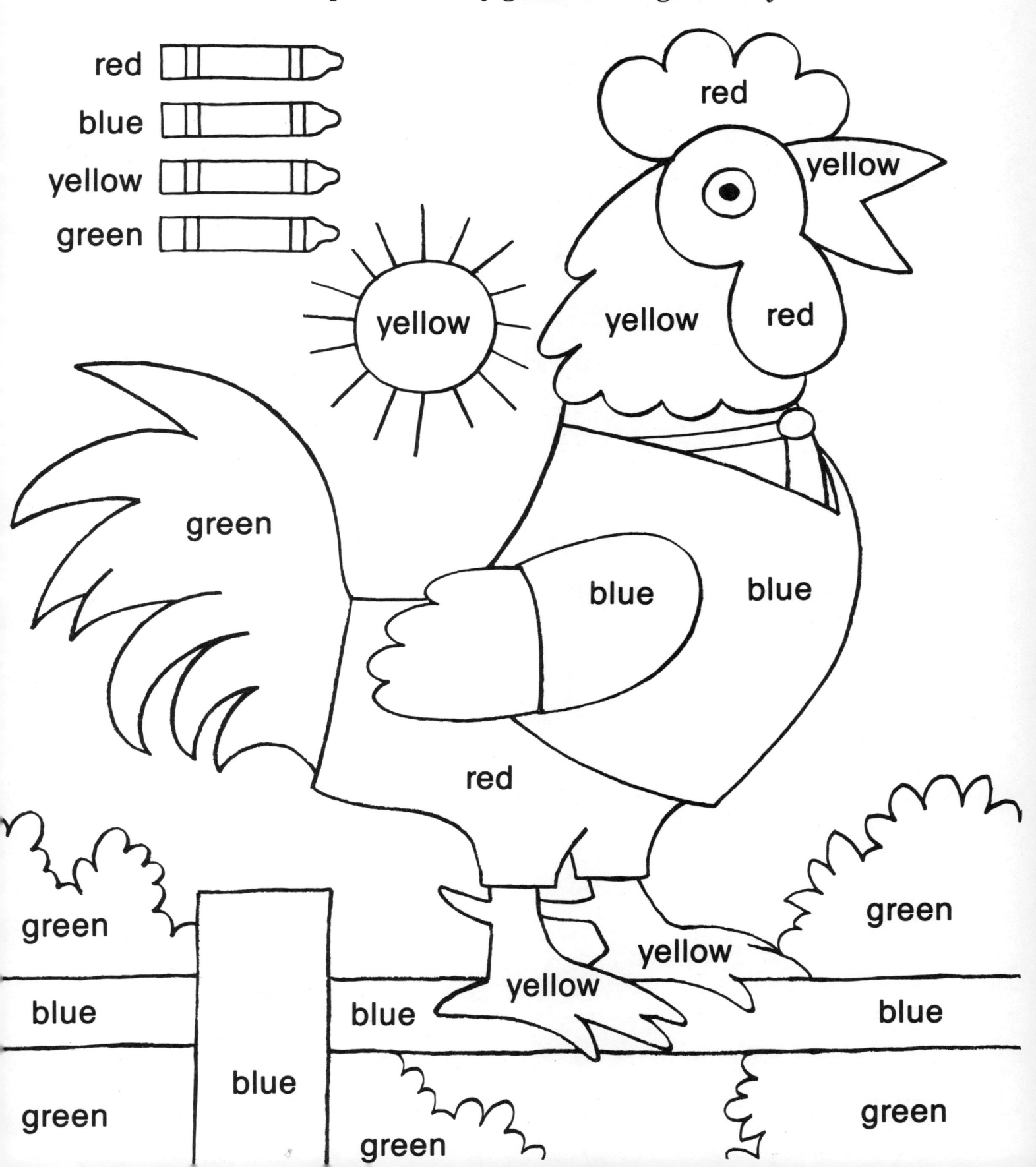

red
blue
yellow
green

red
yellow
yellow
red
yellow
green
blue
blue
red
green
yellow
yellow
green
blue
blue
blue
blue
green
green
green

Find the words in the box below. Draw a circle around each word.

cat   pig   run   hat   bed   coat

```
b r c a t s t p i g
x r u n b l h a t m
x b e d w c o a t r
```

Write each word under the correct picture.

Read the words. Say the words. Write the words.

Here Here   Is Is

here here   is is

Here is a 🐛 and a ▱.
          bug   rug

Here is a bug and a rug.

Here is a cat

and a bug on a rug.

The cat and the bug run on the rug.

Read the words. Say the words. Write the words.

big　big　　little　little

The big bear

The big bear can run.

Here is a little mouse.

Here is a little mouse.

The big bear and the little mouse.

Is the mouse little?

A little house

house

The little mouse has
a little house.

A big book.

A little book.

The big bear has a little book.

The little mouse has a big book.

Find the words in the box below. Draw a circle around each word.

bear   mug   book   bell   house   dog

```
h r b e a r u m u g b
n b o o k f s b e l l
h o u s e v w d o g r
```

Write each word under the correct picture.

22

Read the words. Say the words. Write the words.

up

up down

down

in

in

out

out

over

over

under

under

23

Read the number words. Say the number words. Write the words.

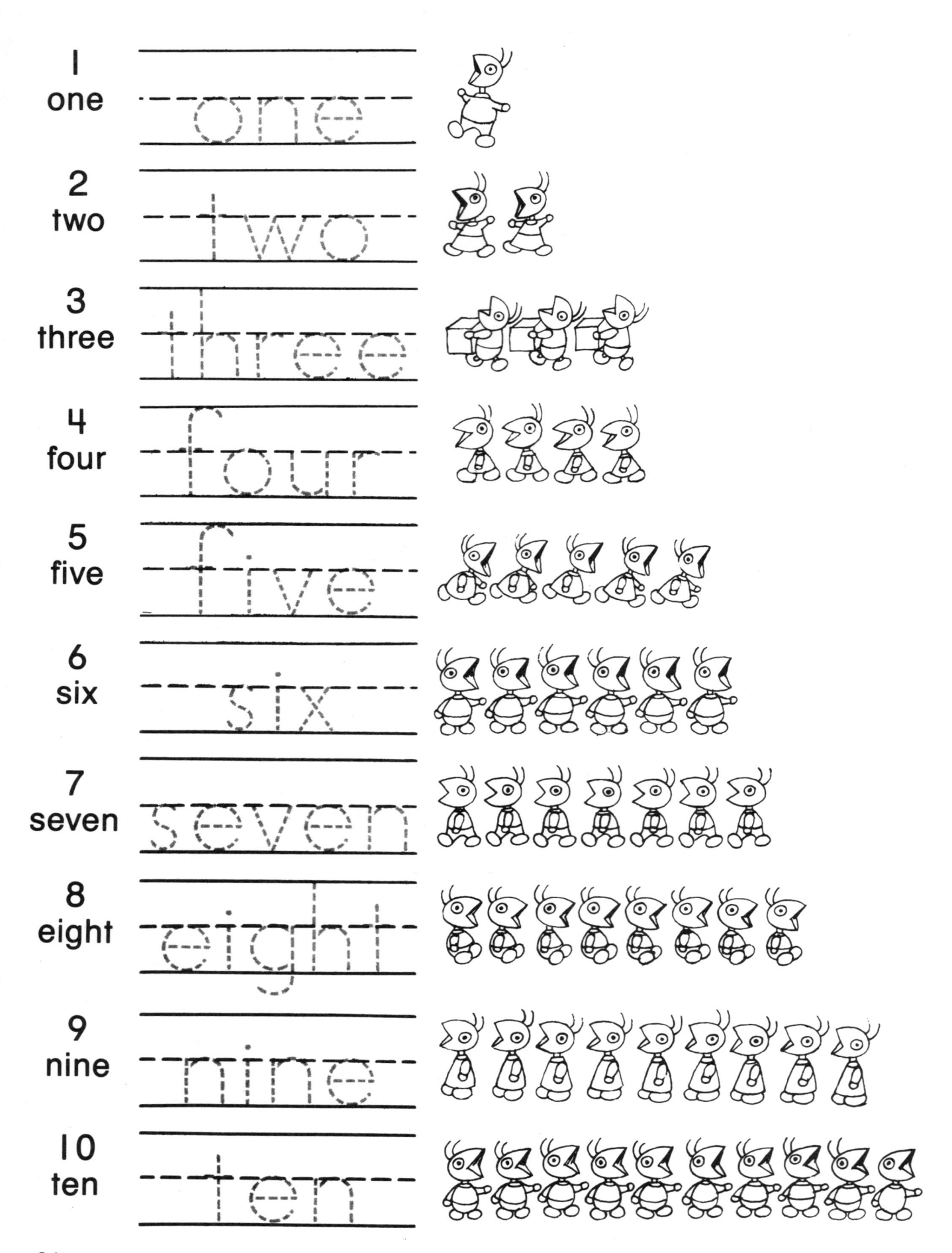

1 one — one

2 two — two

3 three — three

4 four — four

5 five — five

6 six — six

7 seven — seven

8 eight — eight

9 nine — nine

10 ten — ten

Find the number words in the box below. Draw a circle around each word.

two five three six nine eight

```
m r t w o t s f i v e n
v t h r e e b h s i x m
w h n i n e o e i g h t
```

Count. Write the number word under the correct picture.

25

Jump *Jump* jump *jump*

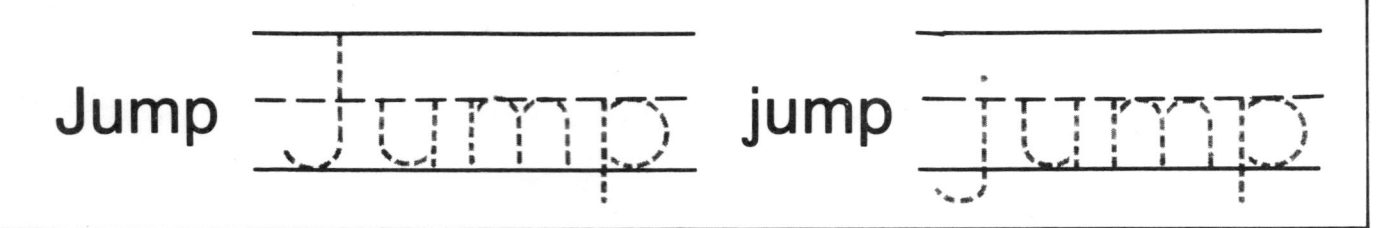

The cat can jump.

One, two, three, four, five.

The pig can jump up and down.

Here is a rabbit.

The *rabbit* can jump.

Run and jump.

Jump over the cat.

Read the words. Say the words. Write the words.

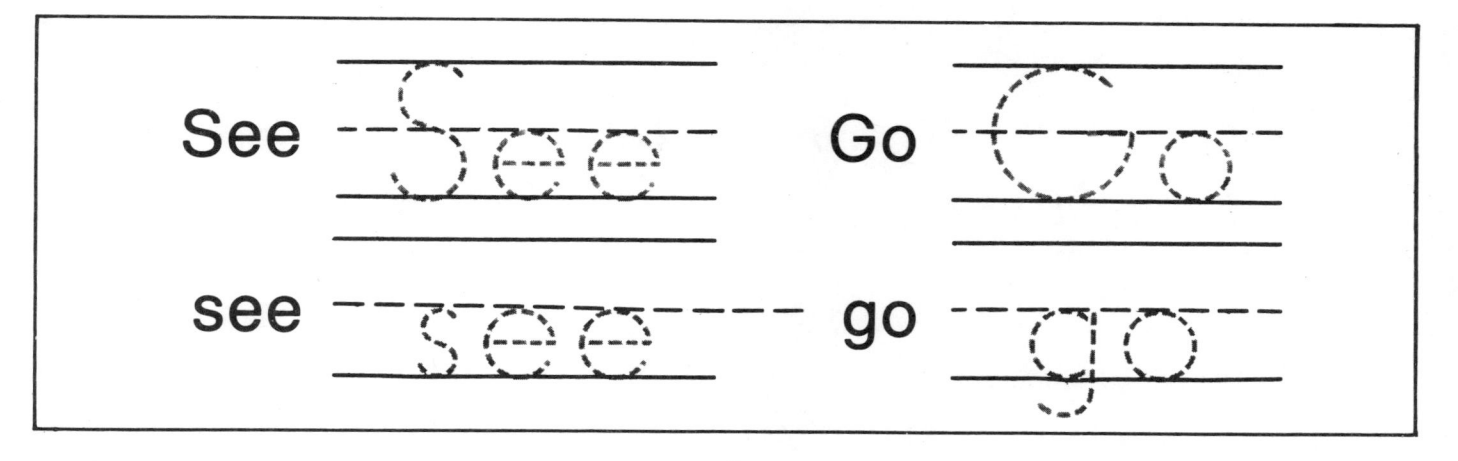

See   See   Go   Go

see   see   go   go

See the bird go up.

See the bird go down.

The rabbit can see five cars.

One, two, three, four, five.

Go, cars, go!

Read the words. Say the words. Write the words.

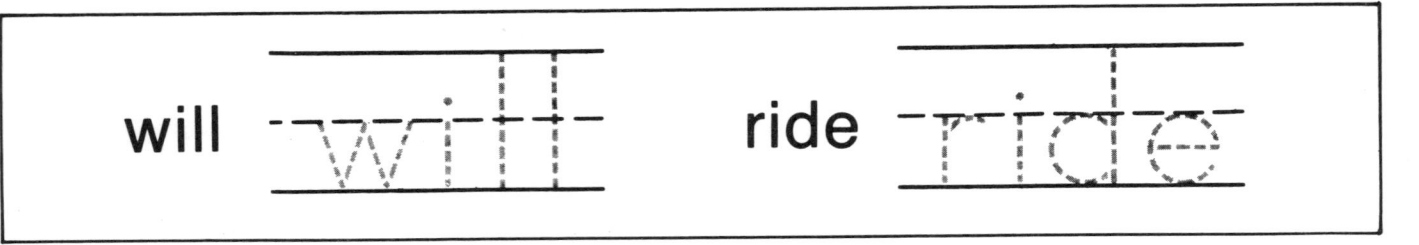

| will | _will_ | ride | _ride_ |

The mouse will go in the little house.

Will the cat ride the bike?

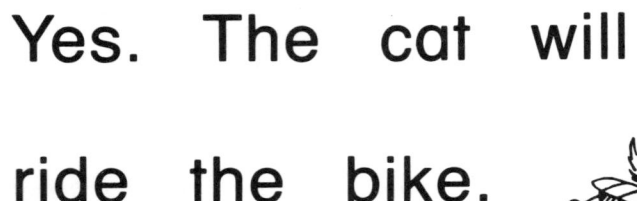

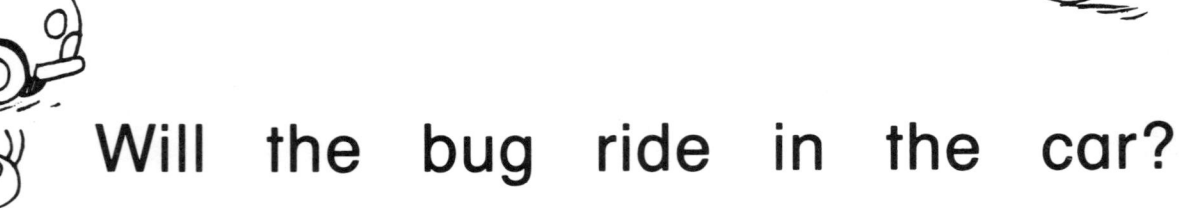

Yes. The cat will ride the bike.

Will the bug ride in the car?

No. The bug will ride in the wagon.

Draw a line under the words that tell about the picture.

The bug is big.

The pig is big.

The mouse is down.

The mouse is up.

The bear can run.

The cat can run.

The dog can see two.

The dog can see four.

Read the words under each box. Draw a picture about the words.

A big cat.

A bug in a car.

A pig and a mouse.

A dog in a hat.

Draw an X on the 8 things that are wrong in the picture.

31

Read the words. Do you see them in the picture? Draw an X on them.

The three pigs ride in a car.

The cat is on the house.

The bug runs after the bear.

The rabbit has a rug.

The dog has a bat and a ball.